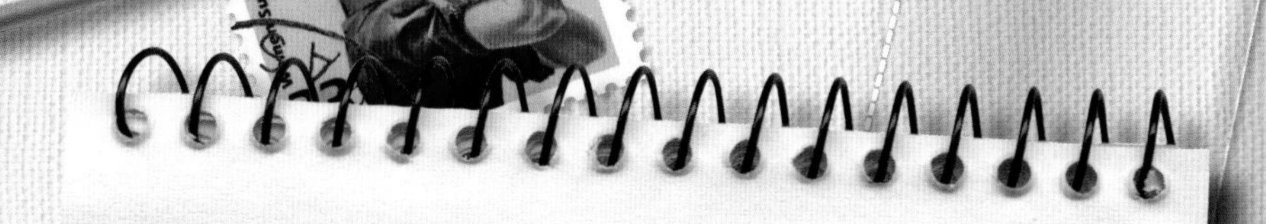

Research It!

The Changing Role of Women Since 1900

Louise Spilsbury

Heinemann Library
Chicago, Illinois

www.heinemannraintree.com
Visit our website to find out more information about Heinemann-Raintree books.

To order:
Phone 888-454-2279
Visit www.heinemannraintree.com to browse our catalog and order online.

Edited by Andrew Farrow and Rebecca Vickers
Designed by Steven Mead
Picture research by Ruth Blair
Production by Victoria Fitzgerald
Originated by Capstone Global Library Ltd
Printed and bound in China by South China Printing Company Ltd

14 13 12 11 10
10 9 8 7 6 5 4 3 2 1

Library of Congress Cataloging-in-Publication Data
Spilsbury, Louise.
The changing role of women since 1900 / Louise Spilsbury.
p. cm. -- (Research it!)
Includes bibliographical references and index.
ISBN 978-1-4329-3496-5 (hc)
1. Women--History. 2. Women--History--Research. I. Title.
HQ1121.S63 2009
305.4209--dc22

2009008758

Acknowledgments
The author and publishers are grateful to the following for permission to reproduce copyright material: Alamy: pp. **51** (© Grapheast), **49** (© INTERFOTO Pressebildagentur), **15** (© David Noton Photography), **43** (© RFStock), **13** (© Michael Ventura); © Corbis: p. **39** (Bettmann); Getty Images: pp. **16** (Ramzi Haidar/AFP), **14**, **37** (Hulton Archive), **27** (Popperfoto); Mary Evans Picture Library: p. **31**; © The National Archives: p. **33** left; © National Portrait Gallery, London: p. **33** right; PA Photos: p. **41** (Dennis Cook/AP); © Rex Features: pp. **5**, **11** (Design Pics Inc), 10 (Roger-Viollet); © shutterstock and © iStockphoto: design features and b/g images.

The main cover image of the suffragette protest is reproduced with permission of Corbis/Bettmann, and the main cover image of the suffragette magazine is reproduced with permission of Corbis/Michael Nicholson. The background images are reproduced with the permission of the following: © iStockphoto (© Olena Druzhynina, © Boros Emese, © Clifford Mueller, © Bill Noll) and © shutterstock (© Sascha Burkard, © Lars Lindblad, © Al Mueller, © Picsfive).

The publisher would like to thank the United Nations Organization for permission to reproduce the web page on page 23. This was downloaded on March 30, 2009.

We would like to thank Stewart Ross for his invaluable help in the preparation of this book.

Contents

Some words are printed in bold, **like this**. You can find out what they mean by looking in the glossary.

Researching Women's History

The role and status of women changed more rapidly in the **western world** during the 20th century than in any other period of history. In 1900 few women had the **right** to vote in elections, and most were not in control of their own lives and instead were treated as secondary to their husbands, fathers, and even brothers! Over the course of the 20th century, which saw two world wars and dramatic advances in transportation, technology, and communications, women's roles altered dramatically. By 2000 most women had gained the right to vote, and many had gained a more independent life than women a century earlier would have believed possible.

However, there is still much debate about whether all the changes, or the impacts of those changes, are necessarily positive, and there is still a long way to go to win equal rights for all the world's women. Around the globe, women's roles are still changing, making this a very relevant and exciting history topic to research and study.

Why research?

People research because they want to find out things for themselves. You may choose a topic like this to research out of your own interest, or because you need to find information to help you write an essay or report, answer test questions, or make an oral presentation. Researching women's history is challenging. Until the early 1970s, women's history was not really a subject that was studied. Topics such as women's **suffrage** (right to vote) were only just mentioned in most history textbooks. This book provides some of the facts, but to fill in gaps in your knowledge you will need to carry out your own research.

We can research and find out about the past from the wealth of information available in books, on the Internet, and from many other sources. This can be a bit like looking for a needle in a haystack, so this book will look at the techniques and approaches you will need to research and answer questions about the changing role of women since 1900. In addition to helping you find information, it will also explain some of the research skills you will need to sort, evaluate, and understand that information.

Research challenges

Your research challenge may be to answer a variety of questions about women's changing role and status in the 20th century. Here are a few examples:

- What changes helped bring about the 19th amendment, which gave women over 21 the right to vote in the United States starting in 1920?
- How significant was the impact of the two world wars on the role and status of women?
- How did opportunities for women change from 1900 to 2000?

Don't think of research as a boring thing to do. One way to bring history research alive is to get firsthand accounts of the past, perhaps from older relatives or friends. Ask women what their and their mothers' lives were like in the past. What changes have they experienced in their lifetimes, and what is their opinion of those changes?

Understanding information

One reason you can now find an enormous amount of research information on the topic of women's changing role in history is because it is a topic about which people have strong views. This means that sometimes the books or other sources that you read will contain attitudes and opinions as well as facts.

For example, a historian may focus only on the way women were **oppressed** and not mention the positive aspects of their lives at a particular time or in a particular place. This may represent a **biased** view. That is why it is important to use more than one source to find out about a person or event in the past when researching a history topic like this one. To be able to get a full picture of the past, you will need to understand and extract information from different kinds of sources and also cross-check and confirm dates and other kinds of information.

The research process

You can think of the research process as eight simple steps, which we will look at in more depth throughout the book. If you follow these steps, you cannot go too far off track:

Step 1 Gain an overview. Get an idea of the topic in a wider context.
Step 2 Decide what you need to know. Link your research to your question or study topic.
Step 3 Research by using many sources, including books and the Internet.
Step 4 Look at images and learn how to "read" them and how to use them.
Step 5 Make thorough and well-referenced research notes.
Step 6 Evaluate your research.
Step 7 Organize your research notes.
Step 8 Present your findings.

A variety of sources

Research gives you a chance to use a variety of sources of information. Generally there are two kinds of source: primary and secondary. **Primary sources** are original, firsthand accounts of events, such as official documents like prison records or wills created at the time the historical events occurred,

artifacts (objects that existed at the time), and sources such as letters, diaries, and newspaper reports written by people at the time of an event or not long after it happened.

Secondary sources are those created after an event, and that have usually been created using different primary sources. They often mention primary sources or use **quotations** from them. Secondary sources include history textbooks and biographies of famous people. Because secondary sources are often published books, they are usually easier to find than primary sources. Ideally, you will use a wide mix of primary and secondary sources in your research.

Types of source

PRIMARY	SECONDARY
Diaries/memoirs	History textbooks
Letters	Biographies
Photographs	Journal articles
News footage	Academic works
Sound recordings	Encyclopedias
Newspaper stories	TV documentaries
Eyewitness accounts	Movies
Military reports	
Government reports	

When were they made?

PRIMARY	SECONDARY
At the time of an event, or very soon after	Created after an event; sometimes a long time after something happened

Who created them?

PRIMARY	SECONDARY
Someone who saw or heard an event himself or herself; these sources may express an opinion or argument about a past event	Someone who wasn't there, often using a range of primary or other secondary sources; these sources may express an opinion or argument about a past event

How common are they?

PRIMARY	SECONDARY
Often one-of-a-kind, or rare	More commonly available

How Has the Role of Women Changed?

The history of women's rights, or their role and status in society, is a challenging topic to research because it can be looked at from so many different angles—by country, by time period, by themes such as politics or education, or by famous or important personalities. That is why a good place to start your research is with general reference sources, such as an encyclopedia or general history books (in print or online). These will help you to get an overview of the general topic or a particular period. If you do not know a great deal about your subject, an overview provides you with a basic understanding of it and a platform from which to extend your research. This will help you think about what else you need to look for online or in print at the next stage. When doing your own research, you will come across some of the themes and topics that follow.

From the 1900s

Your starting point for research could be that in 1900 most women across the world had few rights. Few had the right to vote in general elections, and in many countries the woman's realm was the home. Women were responsible for caring for children and doing household work, such as cleaning and cooking, in their own homes or for other people. Most middle-class women left home only when they married, and then everything they owned was transferred from their fathers to their husbands. Divorce was not an option for most women, no matter how unhappy or abusive their marriages were.

In 1900 there was no welfare system and also limited healthcare. Many women were weakened by frequent pregnancies, and large numbers died in childbirth because they did not have proper medical care.

Many women did not have access to education, and those who did usually did not get the same educational opportunities as boys. For others, education was considered a waste of time because they were destined to be wives and mothers. Although a few rich women trained and worked as doctors or in other professions, throughout the world most women worked in the fields, as servants, or in manual labor jobs, for long hours and for low or no wages.

The birth of women's rights

Before 1900 there had already been many calls for change. During the French Revolution, a writer and political activist, Olympe de Gouge, published her *Declaration of the Rights of Woman and the Female Citizen* (1791). In Great Britain in 1792, Mary Wollstonecraft wrote *A Vindication of the Rights of Woman*, a book that argued for educational and social rights for women. In 1848 in the United States, women's rights activist Elizabeth Cady Stanton presented the *Declaration of Rights and Sentiments* at a historic women's rights convention in Seneca Falls, New York. This document demanded that women be allowed to take an equal part in society alongside men, including the right to vote in elections. Stanton and another campaigner, Susan B. Anthony, founded the U.S. National Women Suffrage Association in 1869. In Australia, Vida Goldstein actively promoted women's rights and founded the National Council of Women in 1888.

Individual women had also made progress by challenging society's standards. For example, at a time when it was unheard of for women to be doctors, in 1849 Elizabeth Blackwell became the first woman to earn a medical degree in the United States. In 1896 Mary Church Terrell led a group of African-American women to form the National Association of Colored Women. The group sought rights for African-American women during a period when both women and African-Americans were treated by the law as unequal. The group fought for issues of concern for African-American women such as suffrage, desegregation, and education.

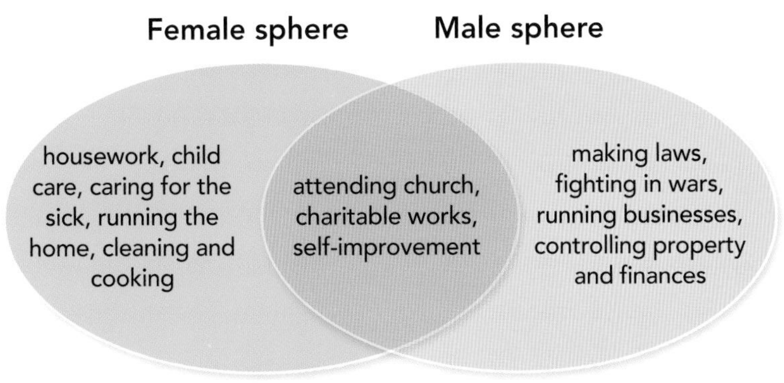

Female sphere | **Male sphere**

housework, child care, caring for the sick, running the home, cleaning and cooking

attending church, charitable works, self-improvement

making laws, fighting in wars, running businesses, controlling property and finances

Venn diagrams like this one are useful for comparing and contrasting information. This one shows the differences in the upper-middle class between the private female sphere of influence and responsibility and the public male sphere that still dominated in 1900. The area in the middle shows areas where both women and men had similar responsibilities.

Suffragettes and suffragists

An important theme in the study of women's changing role during the early years of the 20th century is the struggle for women's suffrage—the right to vote. This would allow women to influence governments who made decisions about their lives. Women who campaigned for suffrage were called **suffragists** or **suffragettes**. The suffragists had more members and held meetings and peaceful processions.

The suffragettes had fewer members, but are more renowned because they carried out more extreme protests. In the United Kingdom, a minority of suffragettes chained themselves to railings, broke windows, and ended up in prison. The *Daily Mail* newspaper in January 1906 dubbed these women "suffragettes" as a term of abuse, but many women in the United Kingdom and United States defiantly adopted the term. The movement for women's suffrage developed around the world, in women's associations in China, India, and Egypt, for example, and in many places with the support of men.

Throughout western Europe, women were campaigning for the vote. This demonstration was held in Paris, France, in 1914.

The impact of World War I

With the outbreak of World War I in 1914, the struggle for suffrage was put on hold because most suffragettes (and suffragists) joined the war effort—for example, by helping to recruit young men to the army. In spite of the reduction in direct campaigning for suffrage at this time, many people believe that the changes in women's role during the war helped them to achieve the vote after the war was over. When men left to fight in the war, industries in their home countries required workers, and women stepped in. Women worked in many industries they would never have been able to before, from weapons factories to public transportation, government offices, or shipbuilding.

After the war ended in 1918, these same women lost their jobs to make way for the men coming back home, but attitudes toward women and their rights had shifted, and around the world women gained the vote. In the Soviet Union and countries in eastern Europe, communist revolutions brought hardships, but they granted women equal rights, too, often long before women in the West won such rights. In 1918 the Soviet Union introduced **maternity leave**, government-funded child care, equal pay for equal work, equal education, and the right to hold political office.

During World War I, women filled many positions brought into existence by wartime needs. Women were welcomed into jobs and industries that had previously excluded them. In some countries this changed immediately after the war was over. For example, in the United States, many women were laid off of their jobs when male soldiers returned home and needed employment. Some states even banned women from taking "men's jobs" after the war.

Women's suffrage victories

Here are some dates from around the world when women gained the right to vote in at least some elections:

- **1893** New Zealand
- **1902** Australia (except Aboriginal peoples)
- **1906** Finland
- **1915** Denmark
- **1917** Soviet Union, Canada
- **1918** Germany, the Netherlands, Great Britain (women age 30 and over)
- **1920** United States
- **1932** Ceylon (now Sri Lanka)
- **1934** Brazil
- **1944** Jamaica, France
- **1945** Italy, Japan
- **1949** China, India
- **1952** Mexico
- **1956** Egypt
- **1964** Kenya
- **1971** Switzerland
- **1974** Jordan

Between the wars

In spite of initial setbacks, after the end of World War I, the 1920s brought new freedoms and changes for many women in terms of work and advances in women's education. More universities opened to women, and more women gained college degrees than ever before. In 1928, U.S. women earned 39 percent of college degrees, compared to 19 percent in 1900.

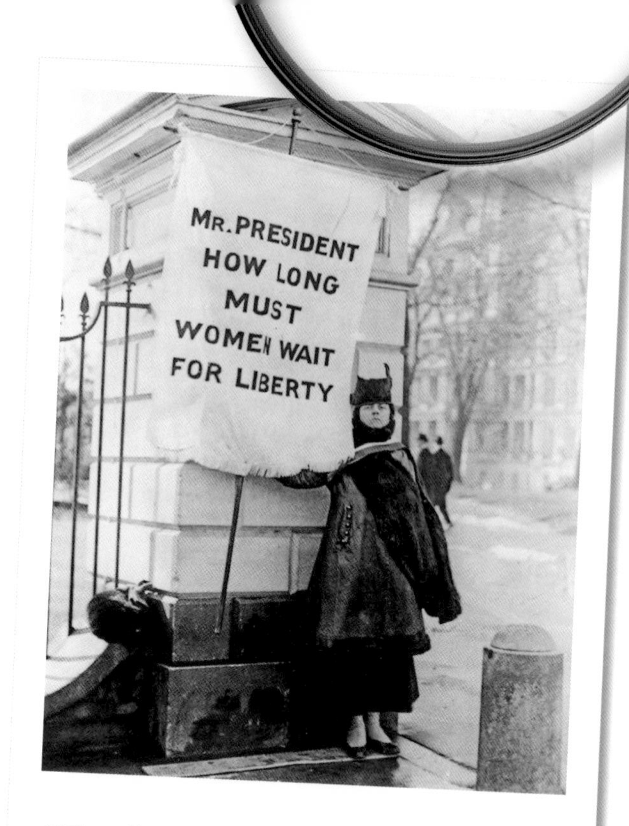

U.S. suffragettes and campaigners for women's rights often picketed the White House and other government buildings in Washington, D.C.

The issue of women's access to **contraception** also came to the fore when Margaret Sanger set up the first **birth-control** clinic in the United States in 1916, and Marie Stopes opened a birth-control clinic in London in 1921. Although few women had access to these clinics, it was the beginning of a major change that would allow women more freedom to pursue their own careers and goals. Another change was in the world of sports. In 1900 women were expected to do "ladylike" sports, such as dancing and horse-riding. In the 1928 Olympics, women were finally allowed to compete in gymnastics and athletics events.

World War II

During World War II (1939–1945), women played an even more active role than they had in World War I. In addition to taking on men's work in their home countries, many women joined the armed services— for example, as pilots in the United States, United Kingdom, and Soviet Union. To make it easier for women to work, nurseries were set up to look after children while their mothers were out, and part-time work was introduced in several countries so that women could fit work in with their other responsibilities at home. However, women were still paid less than men for doing the same work.

Defining "women's work"

After World War II, some governments expected women to return home and leave the jobs free for men who were returning from war. In some countries, women came under pressure from politicians to stay at home to have more children to help rebuild the economy after the war. More babies meant more demand for goods and services, and more workers and consumers for the future. In France, the government introduced a series of allowances that were given to women according to how many children they had. This was not the case in countries such as the Soviet Union, where women continued to work in many areas, such as engineering and manual labor, deemed "men's work" in the West. Today, the definition of what jobs are suitable for women is still hotly debated. For example, in some armies, women fight on the front line alongside men in war situations, but some officers and civilians argue that women are not physically or emotionally suited to the front line and should leave this "work" to men.

The 1960s and 1970s

In 1963 a landmark book called *The Feminine Mystique* by U.S. feminist Betty Friedan was published. Dedicated to French feminist and philosopher Simone de Beauvoir, who first used the term "women's liberation," Friedan called for women to look beyond the role of homemaker. She wasn't alone. In the West during the 1960s and 1970s, the "women's liberation" political movement campaigned on a number of issues, such as equal pay and equal rights at work. Among the most active groups was the National Organization of Women (NOW), which was formed in 1966 in the United States.

Many more women joined the workforce during this period. For example, in the United States the number increased to 43 percent in 1969, compared to 25 percent in 1940, although women's wages were still only 60 percent of men's. Also, in the 1960s laws were passed that made it easier for couples to get divorced. The 1960s saw more women taking important government roles. In 1960 Sirimavo Bandaranaike became the first democratically elected female national leader when she became prime minister in Sri Lanka, followed by Indira Gandhi in India in 1966, and Golda Meir in Israel in 1969.

Sirimavo Bandaranaike ran for office in Sri Lanka in 1960 after her husband, who had been prime minister, was assassinated. Here she is shown campaigning on behalf of the Freedom Party.

Politics and education today

Today, most women around the world have the right to vote, and many take important roles in government and politics. In Rwanda, women make up about half the government. However, women still do not have the vote in a handful of countries, including Saudi Arabia, and worldwide women hold only 14 percent of parliamentary seats. In terms of education, a much higher percentage of girls and women today go to school and college than in 1900. However, 800 million people worldwide are still **illiterate**, and almost two-thirds of these are women. An interesting avenue for research might be to compare and contrast the status of women in different countries with your own or with others. For example, did you know that in Iran more than 65 percent of college students are women, or that in Africa more than 40 percent of women do not have access to even the most basic education?

A woman's right to choose?

In the 1960s, NOW and many other feminist groups fought for legal **abortions**, which they said was about a woman's right to choose whether or not to have a child. By the 1970s, women had been granted restricted rights to abortion in the West, but this remains a hotly debated issue around the world, as those against abortion say they are defending the rights of the unborn child. Many people argue that a more important issue is that many women do not have adequate medical care, especially during pregnancy. Globally, over half a million women die in pregnancy and childbirth every year, and 99 percent of these deaths occur in developing countries. The contraceptive pill, available since the 1960s, gave women the ability to choose when and whether to have children. One research line to follow could be to find out about the influence and profile of prominent campaigners for women's right to choose, such as Gloria Steinem (who also cofounded the feminist magazine *Ms.* in 1972).

Women's status today

Some women—including Helen Greiner, cofounder and board member of iRobot, the largest robot company in the world—do succeed in business. However, across the globe women are still paid less than men in general, and still hold only a small proportion of the senior jobs in influential careers such as business, politics, and the law. And it is not simply the case that women fare better in the West: in 2008 only 17 percent of members of the U.S. Congress were women, compared to 27.7 percent in Afghanistan and 25.5 percent in Iraq. The difficulties some women have combining motherhood and work, such as child-care problems, sharing domestic chores, and discrimination against working mothers, would make an interesting research topic.

*According to the **UN**, women work two-thirds of the world's working hours and produce half of the world's food. Yet they earn only 10 percent of the world's income and own less than 1 percent of the world's property.*

Timeline

This timeline shows a selection of significant dates in the history of women's changing role in the 20th century:

Date	Event
1900	Suffragists start to campaign in many parts of the world.
1902	Women in Australia get the vote.
1903	The U.S. National Women's Trade Union League (WTUL) is established to advocate the rights of women in the workplace.
1916	Women over 30 in the United Kingdom get the right to vote.
1916	Margaret Sanger opens the first U.S. birth-control clinic, in Brooklyn, New York.
1920	Women 21 and over in the United States get the right to vote.
1928	Women compete for the first time in Olympic field events.
1932	Amelia Earhart is the first woman to fly solo over the Atlantic Ocean.
1944	Women in France get the right to vote.
1953	*The Second Sex* by French feminist writer Simone De Beauvoir is published in the United States (first published in France in 1949); it contains the first use of the phrase "women's liberation."
1960	Sirimavo Bandaranaike of Sri Lanka is the first democratically elected female national leader.
1960	The U.S. Food and Drug Administration approves the use of birth-control pills.
1963	Russian Lt. Col. Valentina Tereshkova is the first woman in space.
1963	Betty Friedan publishes *The Feminine Mystique*.
1963	The U.S. Congress passes the Equal Pay Act, requiring employers to pay a woman the same as a man for doing the same job.
1966	The U.S. National Organization for Women (NOW) is founded.
1966	Indira Gandhi becomes the first female prime minister of India.
1969	Golda Meir becomes the first female prime minister of Israel.
1972	The U.S. Congress passes the Equal Rights Amendment (ERA), which guarantees that equal rights can never be denied on the basis of sex. However, not enough states **ratify** the amendment.
1972	The feminist magazine *Ms.*, cofounded by Gloria Steinem, is launched.
1973	In the decision *Roe v. Wade*, the U.S. Supreme Court establishes a woman's right to a safe abortion.
1974	The U.S. Coalition of Labor Union Women (CLUW) is founded by women labor union leaders aiming to increase women's involvement in unions.
1975	The United Nations' Decade for Women begins; the UN runs several conferences to examine women's living conditions around the world.
1979	Margaret Thatcher is elected the first UK female prime minister.
1988	Benazir Bhutto becomes the first female prime minister of Pakistan.
1993	The first "Take Our Daughters to Work Day" is held in the United States.
1997	Madeleine Albright becomes the first female U.S. secretary of state.
2003	Iranian lawyer and human rights activist Shirin Ebadi is awarded the Nobel Peace Prize for her efforts for the rights of women and children.
2005	Angela Merkel becomes Germany's first woman chancellor.

Challenges facing women's status

Women's status is still at issue in many places—for example, in countries where tradition and/or religious beliefs can be a barrier to equal rights. Here are a few examples:

- Under the Muslim law of inheritance, a daughter is eligible for only half the share of property given to a son.
- In Pakistan, men are entitled to take the law into their own hands for the sake of the family's "honor" and murder wives, daughters, or sisters they suspect of adultery.
- In Afghanistan, women are murdered for working or campaigning on women's rights issues.
- In parts of some countries where families favor male children, including India and China, many female babies are killed at birth because they are considered of low worth.

For some people, progress means allowing women to have the rights to do what men do, such as fighting on equal terms in the armed forces. However, many think real progress would consist of making the world a better, more peaceful place for both sexes.

Making a Start

When you research a topic, you need to start out by collecting background evidence and information, such as specific dates and events. That way you can piece together your own understanding of the subject. In this chapter we look at where you can find information and how to research in a successful, focused way.

The long and short of it

First, take a moment to reread the question or assignment that you have been given. Check the terms of the question or assignment. To find out how much information you will need to research, check if the project requires a short, medium, or long answer. Use a highlighter to highlight key numbers or words, such as the dates you are meant to cover or the main issue you should discuss. For example, does the assignment ask you to cover just the war years, or does it focus on a single issue, such as equal pay? This helps to focus your mind on the job at hand.

What do you know?

Whenever you are about to learn something new, it helps to start with what you already know. One way to do this is by brainstorming. Brainstorming is when you give yourself a set time to jot down anything you know that is related to the topic. There are no right or wrong answers, and you should feel free just to write down anything and everything that comes into your head. When you review the brainstorming notes later, you may reject some ideas as irrelevant, but you should find that others help to set you off on your research journey.

KWL charts

Another way to organize what you need to find out is through a KWL chart. The K stands for "What I **K**now," the W for "What I **W**ant to Know," and the L for "What I **L**earned." The first two columns should be completed before you start your research. The third column should be completed after the research is done. The charts help you to find specific things to look for, and when you fill in the final column after your research is finished, it helps you to reflect on what you have learned.

What I **K**now	What I **W**ant to know	What I **L**earned
Suffragettes fought for women's rights. *Alice Paul was a famous suffragette.* *Some suffragettes protested by chaining themselves to railings.*	*Who opposed women's suffrage and why?* *Why was she called a suffragette?* *Why did they protest in that way?* *Were the suffragettes successful?*	*[to be completed later]*

This KWL chart was made in response to the question "Who were the suffragettes, and what did they do?"

Narrowing and broadening your topic

Sometimes in a question for an essay or report, you may be given a very broad research topic, such as "How did women's roles change between 1900 and 2000?" This covers an overwhelming amount of information, so it is best if you break the topic down into several smaller, more manageable topics. For example, a broad topic like women's changing role could be broken down into different areas like education or equal pay or the right to vote. You could also narrow a topic down in terms of place or time. On the other hand, you may need to research a specific, narrow question such as "Who was Alice Paul?" It may then help to broaden your research to understand the context of this person or event. For example, you might research the key events she was involved in and what changes she saw in her lifetime to see how she fitted into the wider history.

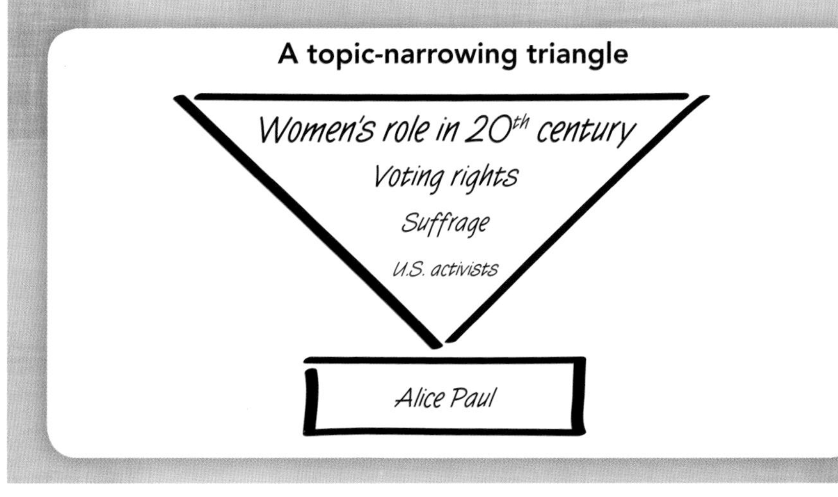

Starting your research

Once you know what you want to find out, the best place to start your research is the library. Unlike many pages on the Internet (see pages 22–23), information books in a library have been checked by editors, publishers, and the librarian. Although they may not be perfect, there have been quality checks, so you can trust that the information is fairly accurate. Search for reference books in your subject area, specifically those about women's history. Also look at general history books that cover the time period you are interested in, or search a library catalog to find books on your topic.

Contents

In this history book about women in the 20th century, a quick look down the contents list shows that you can find a reference to votes for women on page 6. Would any of the other pages be useful or of interest?

Finding your way

Once you have a history book in your hand, you will want to find relevant information quickly and efficiently. An encyclopedia may be organized alphabetically or by subject, so you could flick through to "W" to see if there is a feature on "women's rights," or "S" for "suffragettes." Otherwise, the contents list is usually your first stop. This lists the chapters or sections of a book in the order in which they appear.

Sanger, Margaret 22
Seneca Falls conference 5
segregation in United States 12
sexual harassment 33
Soviet Union 9, 33
Stanton, Elizabeth Cady 5
suffrage 6, 8, 9
suffragettes and suffragists 6, 7, 24

Thatcher, Margaret 11
trade unions 28, 31, 32-33, 35

Check the index at the back of a history book to see if the book has any information about a specific person or event you are studying—for example, a figure such as Elizabeth Cady Stanton or Margaret Thatcher. Don't forget that indexes list last names first—for example, Thatcher, Margaret.

Another way of finding out if a book has the information you seek without reading the whole thing is to check the **index**. You will find the index at the back of a book. It is a list of all the names, important events, and subjects covered in the book, and it is laid out in alphabetical order. Pictures, graphs, and charts might be in italics, and some entries will be found under other subheadings. For example, if you are looking for laws about equal pay, you may have to look under the subheading "laws" to find specific laws on women's rights.

Bibliographies

A **bibliography** is a list of books and other sources that an author used in writing a book. The bibliography is usually found at the end of a book. Bibliographies are useful because they may lead you to other useful books. Some bibliographies may be divided into different formats or subjects. Books in a bibliography usually give the author's name (last name first), then the book title and then other details, like the publisher and the date the book was published, to help you find it or order it from the library. To check whether a book is going to be a useful resource for you, look on the Internet for reviews and for more information about what it contains.

Online research

Access to online resources can be made through home, school, or library computers. Most schools have free access to some **databases**. Research databases are developed, and their information selected and checked for accuracy, with a specific audience in mind. As online research databases are often subscription services (where membership or payment is required), schools and public libraries join on behalf of their users. Ask your teacher or a librarian what is available to you, and for any user name or password.

The Internet

The Internet can be a great source of information and gives you access to less well-known, and often interesting, research topics. However, one problem with Internet research is that there is so much material out there. Finding the right information can take hours, and you will have to plow through pages and pages of irrelevant material to get to it.

One way to use the Internet is through search engines, such as Google and Yahoo!, but you need to search in a way that produces helpful results. These methods work on Google and most other search engines:

- You can force Google to exclude words by putting a minus symbol right before them. For example, by using "women -fashion" you can search for pages about women that don't include information about fashion.
- In some search engines you can use "OR" to search for pages that contain either of two terms. For example, the search "women World War II OR WW II OR Second World War" allows for the fact that World War II is written in different ways.
- If you are searching for something very specific, a good tip is to put your phrase or search words in quotation marks. For example, if you type in "Gloria Steinem founded Ms.," the search engine will only list websites that include that exact phrase, rather than all of the websites that include those four words at some point.
- Focus the search by adding other relevant search words. For example, rather than just searching for "women in politics," you could search for "women in politics France."

Quality and accuracy

The quality of information on the Internet varies a lot, and you cannot trust everything. There are obvious reasons for this: anyone can put a page up on the Internet—they might be a professor of women's history or an ordinary person with strong opinions. People can say anything they like and leave it there as long as they like, so you have to be careful about which information you use. For example, there are well-established online encyclopedias, but there are also websites, such as *Wikipedia*, that are written by volunteers who may or may not know what they are talking about.

Understanding a website

Start with major library and museum websites that have special learning sections and follow links from their pages, since these are likely to have been checked. Major organizations, such as the United Nations (see below), have their own websites that carry fact sheets and links. The URL is the web address of the page you are accessing. It appears at the top of your browser when you have a web page open—for example, http://www.si.edu. The letters after the name of the website tell you what sort of organization it is. Look for academic or educational websites that end with .edu. You might also try government sites, which end with .gov. Sites that end with .com are businesses or commercial sites and in general exist to make money, not merely to share information. Check the website for information about who wrote it, where it is from, and when it was written. Cross-check the name of the writer with other things the author has written to find out if he or she is genuinely an expert.

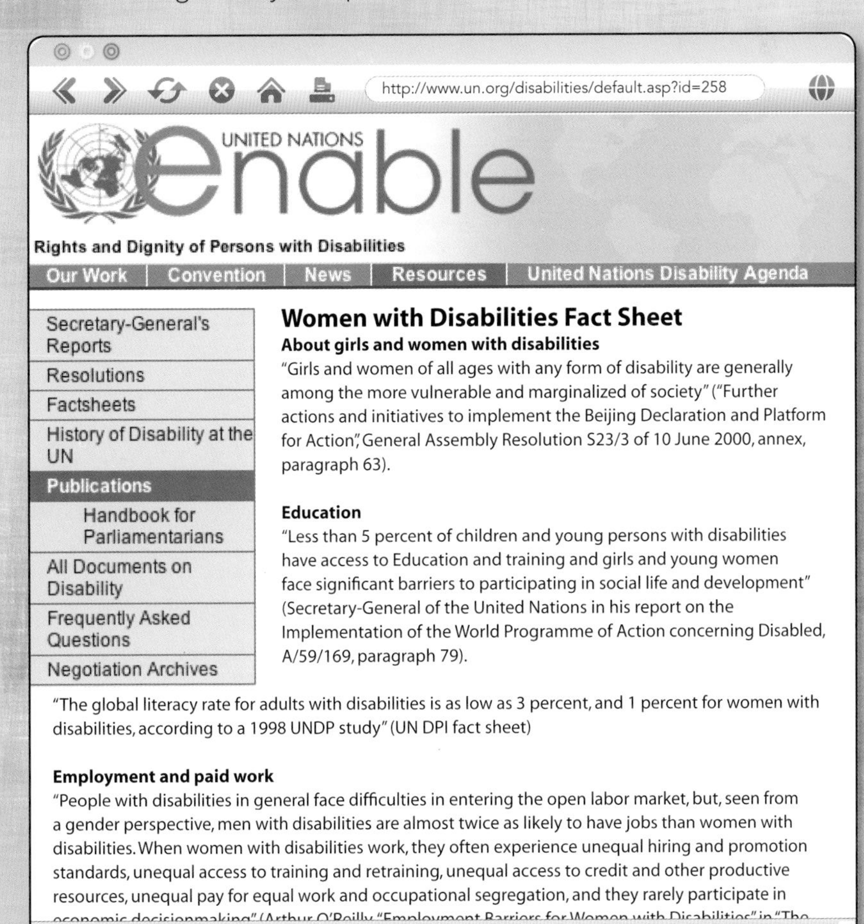

Skimming and scanning for information

When you have narrowed down your research techniques efficiently and found a good article on the Internet or a useful chapter in a library book, you still won't have time to read every word in them. You need to develop skills in **skimming** and **scanning** so you can increase your reading speed and get the most out of a source in the minimum time.

The way to do this is to first be clear about what you are looking for. So, for example, if you are researching a paper on women's role during the two world wars, you might be looking specifically for women in active service in World War II.

Skimming

Then you need to skim the resource to find out what information it contains about your topic. Skimming a resource means looking quickly through the headings, pictures, and first and last sentences of the different sections or paragraphs to get an idea of which parts are useful to you. In this case, you might be looking for words such as "pilots," "front line," or "WAC" (Women's Army Corp), which was the women's branch of the U.S. Army during World War II.

When you skim you should read at about twice your normal reading speed. The idea is to find paragraphs that might be useful, not to read carefully for sense at this stage.

Scanning

Scanning is a technique that helps you locate specific information, such as names, dates, or places within a piece of text. When you scan, you know what you are looking for before you start reading. The idea is that you quickly scan—or glance—down the page, keeping your eye out for a key word or date.

So, for example, imagine you were looking for information about public opinion about women serving as soldiers during World War II. As you quickly run your eyes across and down a page, you don't really read the words. Instead you look out for words that apply to what you are interested in, such as "controversy" or "opposition."

The SQ3R technique

A technique called **SQ3R** can help you to examine, assess, and organize the information that you gain from your research sources. The letters "SQ3R" stand for "**S**urvey, **Q**uestion, **R**ead, **R**ecite, **R**eview." These five steps can be very useful if you are feeling puzzled or overwhelmed by all the information you have found. To use the SQ3R technique, follow these simple steps:

Survey ...

- a work's title, chapter, and spread headings and subheadings, as well as captions to pictures, charts, graphs, and maps.
- the foreword or introduction and conclusion or **summary**, looking for major ideas.
- review questions and educational study guides.

Question

- Turn the title, headings, and subheadings into questions.
- Ask yourself, "What question is this work trying to answer?"
- Read any questions that appear at the end of sections or chapters.
- Ask yourself, "What did my teacher say about this subject or chapter when the project was assigned?"
- Ask yourself, "What do I already know about this subject?"

Read

- Look for answers to the questions that appear at the end of chapters or in an educational study guide.
- Reread captions to pictures, charts, graphs, and maps.
- Note all words or phrases that are underlined, italic, or bold.
- Read difficult passages more slowly.
- Stop and reread any passages that are not clear.
- Read a section at a time.

Recite

- Say questions out loud about what you have just read.
- Take notes from the text, but summarize the information in your own words.
- If using photocopies, underline or highlight important points you have just read.
- Recite answers out loud, remembering that the more sensible your answers, the more likely you are to remember what you read.

Review ...

- the key phrases and other notes you made within 24 hours of making the notes.
- again after one week.
- about once a month until the time of your presentation (or test).

Timelines

What do you do with all those dates you discover over the course of your research? Producing a timeline can be an invaluable way to organize the dates and gain a firm grasp of a new topic. Timelines help you order and visualize a sequence of events. Putting events on a timeline gives you a sense of how much time goes by in between each event. You can often find timelines made by someone else, and it is a quick, visual way to see events in **chronological** order. However, it is much more useful to make one of your own, picking the dates relevant to your research. By doing it yourself, you build up a better overview of the period.

Timeline tips

When doing a timeline for a topic, such as women's changing role, you might like to add a second layer of dates, perhaps above the timeline bar. This could contain dates of major world or national events. This helps you to see at a glance how dates are connected and sets the history of women's rights in a wider context. If you make a timeline that includes important world dates, this can be a real help when answering questions like, "How did national and world events affect the role of women?"

How to make a timeline

1. The first thing to do is decide what your timeline will show. The bigger your topic or longer the period of time it covers, the more information there will be. It is best to have a focused plan to cover one topic in your timeline, like "women and health" or "women in politics."
2. Next you need to decide how you will choose events to include and exclude. Will you cover dates for the world or for just one country? Will you include general events, or only those directly related to your topic?
3. Research and note the dates when the events that you wish to include occurred and write down where you found them. That way you can go back and check if the sources were reliable. Don't just accept the date given by one source. Check the date against other sources, too, to make sure you don't make any mistakes.
4. When you have all your dates, figure out which are the earliest and latest dates that you want to include. These will set the time span.
5. Figure out what size segments your timeline will be divided into. For shorter time spans, you could do yearly segments. For longer periods, you could do 10-year segments.
6. Put the dates on your timeline in chronological order.

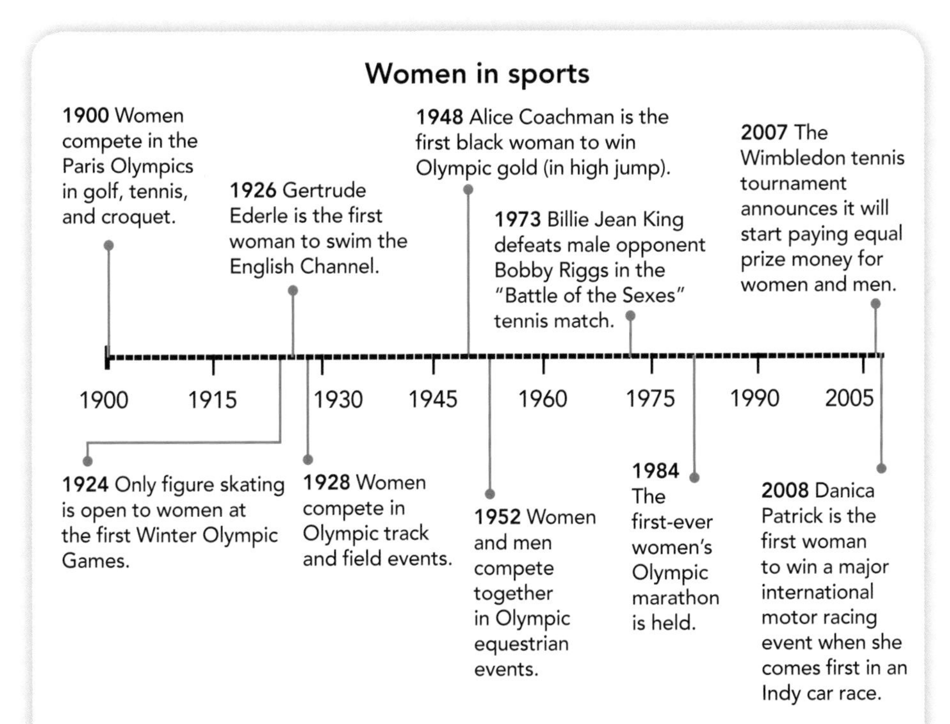

This is an example of a timeline about a specific topic: women in sports.

This picture of some of the women who competed in the 1928 Olympics could be used to illustrate a timeline like the one above.

Record your sources

It is important to keep a note of all the resources you use. When you find a useful source, be sure to write down details, such as the author, title, place, and date of publication. You'll need this information to **cite** the book later, and so that you can check to see if the resource was accurate or to refer to it in an essay. It is a good idea to keep a record of useful sources on note cards (see above). That way, you can add a brief description of what the book or article is about, too.

Ross, Mandy. 20th Century Perspectives: The Changing Role of Women. Chicago: Heinemann Library, 2002.

This book contains information on a wide range of topics. There is one spread on changes since the 1960s on pages 24–25.

Note taking

When you find a useful resource, you might be able to photocopy the page (as long as you mark on it where the information came from), but usually you will take notes about it on cards or sheets. You can do this in several ways:

- Write a summary sentence that sums up what you have learned.
- Use paraphrasing. **Paraphrases** are your own version of information that you have read, and then rewritten in your own words.
- Copy useful sentences of text to use as quotes, as long as you credit the people who said or wrote them.
- Write notes for different topics on different colored cards, or using clear headings on sheets of notes, so that you can see at a glance what topic they cover.

Spreadsheets

One way to combine notes, dates, and lists of sources is in a spreadsheet on a computer. This is when data is stored in a table with rows and columns beneath column headings. Many tables and reports can be stored in the same database file. The table on page 29 is about the attempts to get an Equal Rights Amendment (ERA) in the United States (a law to guarantee equal treatment of men and women in all areas of life) since the 1960s. The U.S. Constitution still remains without an ERA because several states refused to ratify it. You could add extra columns—for example, one for notes on the reliability of the sources.

Source	What does this source show?	How can I use this source?	Where is this source from?
Graph comparing male and female earnings from 1960–2000	In 1960 women earned at least a third less than men.	It shows that women earned less than men. The source also suggests they had lower-status jobs.	U.S. Government Census Bureau records (found on website www.census.gov/prod/2004pubs/p60-226.pdf)
Statement of Purpose from National Women's Organization (NOW) at its first conference in 1966	It shows the aims of the male and female members of NOW.	It shows that men and women were still fighting for equal pay and opportunities in 1966.	At NOW's website, www.now.org/history/purpos66.html
Encyclopedia explanation of the Equal Rights Amendment (ERA) 1972	It shows that the ERA is intended to ban all laws that give one sex different rights than the other.	It tells us the history of the ERA and some of the arguments for and against it.	Online encyclopedia www.worldbook.com
News magazine article from 1980 about a demonstration in Chicago of people demanding that the state of Illinois ratify the ERA	It shows that just because the law was passed, not everyone agreed with it, and some states were slow to ratify it.	It tells us that the members of NOW and other feminists still had to fight for equal rights long after 1972.	*Time* magazine article, May 26, 1980 (www.time.com)

Summing it up: How to research

Here are some tips on how to successfully research your topic:

- First figure out what you know and exactly what it is you want to find out.
- Use as many sources as possible, from the library to the Internet.
- Check that sources are accurate and reliable, especially when using the Internet.
- Keep a full record of all your sources so you can quote from them later.
- Make careful notes in an organized way so that you can retrieve the information later.

Examining Your Sources

How you judge the resources you use in your research is very important. Some people make the mistake of thinking that primary sources, such as newspaper accounts, letters, or photos, are "truer" than secondary sources, such as textbooks written years after the events. However, we must be aware of bias in all resources. Bias is when someone is inclined to favor one view or opinion of an event over alternatives. The person may choose to represent something in a particular way or only present the reader with certain facts, in order to try to influence the reader's opinion one way or the other.

The 5 Ws

To assess whether or not a source is biased in some way, you can use the 5 Ws: What, Who, When, Where, and Why. Asking these five questions about a source can help you determine the accuracy and relevance of the information you have in front of you. There is a difference between fact and opinion, but as this chapter will show, both kinds of resources are valid and useful. The facts that you find, such as dates when laws were passed or organizations were formed, will form the basis of your understanding. However, the many other resources you discover, which may include more opinions than facts, will help you understand why such laws were passed or why some people fought against them.

The 5 Ws approach

What: What is the source? Is it an official document? Does it contain facts or opinions? If facts, have they been chosen to present a particular view?
Who: Who wrote the letter, took the photo, or collected the statistics? What are the writer's motives for creating this message? When you know who created something, can you tell how this might have influenced their choices or writing?
When: When was the source created? How can you tell its age? If it is quite old, could it be out of date?
Where: Can you tell where it was created? If it is a piece about women in China, but was written in the United States, what might that tell you about its accuracy?
Why: Why was the source created? Does the source tell you why it was created? Can you guess why it was created?

Comparing quotes to identify bias

Look at these two quotes. One is from a woman in 1909 and the other from a male politician in 1907. Can you figure out which one is which?

Quote A: *"Women's suffrage is a more dangerous leap in the dark than it was in the 1860s because of the vast growth of the Empire . . . and therewith the increased complexity and risk of the problems which lie before our statesmen . . . problems of men, only to be solved by the labor and special knowledge of men, and where the men who bear the burden ought to be left unhampered by the political inexperience of women."*

Quote B: *"Those who confuse women's character with effeminacy are strangely blind to facts. . . . While her influence in politics will be humanizing it will also be strengthening, and much of the chicanery and knavery [trickery and dishonest behavior] of political life will go down before her direct march upon the actual."*

You may be surprised that Quote A was written by Mary Humphrey Ward (quoted in the London *Times* newspaper in 1909), president of the British Women's National Anti-Suffrage League, who campaigned against women being given the vote. Quote B was written in 1907 by James Keir Hardie, a British politician who supported women's suffrage. Finding out the who, why, when, what, and where of sources helps us understand the bias better.

Artifacts are interesting primary sources, but you still need to ask who made them and when, where, and why they were made. These suffragette badges were worn by women as proud symbols of their determination to gain the vote.

Do photos ever lie?

Photos can be a true and fascinating record of past events. A photograph can sometimes bring an event alive more effectively than words alone, and photographs can add interest and detail to a history report. The very existence of certain photographs can tell us interesting facts about the history of women's changing role. In 2003 the UK National Archives released photographs taken by police who were spying on suffragettes. These prove that the government regarded the suffragettes (who most people today view as heroines) as a terrorist threat. Some of the pictures show women on campaigns and others are "mug shots," pictures used for identification purposes. Some of these mug shots were, for example, circulated to art galleries and museums so they could watch out for "known militant suffragettes" after attacks on some famous works of art.

Using picture sources

While doing your research, you may come across pictures that you would like to use to illustrate your research. You must, however, be aware of **copyright** laws. Students can usually copy and reproduce pictures from the Internet or other sources if they are used purely for their own personal research or in work that is purely for assessment. Otherwise you will need to check the terms of use for any photographs (there may be a link on the homepage of the website where you found the picture). Some sites allow free use, but others do not.

Ways of seeing

When looking at historical photographs, you need to think critically. You need to ask: What is the message that the photo communicates? Does it show the suffragettes in a positive or negative light? Who took the photograph: the police, or a supporter of the suffragette cause? What was the photograph being used for: to present suffragettes as ordinary women, or as terrorists? Many photos show suffragettes chaining themselves to railings, smashing windows, or starting fires. These emphasize the threat the women posed, not the cause for which they fought. There are very few photos that show police and prison brutality against such women, some of whom were force fed using long plastic tubes when on hunger strike, or slapped and beaten. You can also use SQ3R (page 25) or the 5 Ws (page 30) to help you evaluate images.

Altered images

Photographs are rarely totally objective. Photographers can undermine the true facts of an event, and this is often done on purpose. Photographers can choose to show only certain sections of a scene, or even alter prints to give a biased perspective. This can tell us as much about historic events as genuine pictures can.

These photos show a prisoner named Evelyn Manesta. The police wanted prison photos of suffragettes for their records. Some women refused to cooperate and moved to blur the pictures. Manesta was held still by a guard's arm around her neck. In a wanted poster circulated later by the police, the photo was altered. The arm around her neck was cut out and replaced by a scarf.

Letters and diaries

How useful are letters and diaries for researchers? Compared to other kinds of written sources, such as legal records, letters and diaries offer us more personal and individual views of the past. They are also interesting in terms of women's history because they are one of the few sources of information about ordinary people, in contrast to the politicians, businessmen, and other "important" people who usually get their words published. For much of history, women could not achieve positions of power, so their voices were not heard, which makes reading letters and diaries by women even more significant.

Access to ordinary voices

One significant change for many women in the 20th century was the introduction of birth control. In the early 20th century, in addition to deaths in childbirth itself, many women died after being weakened by giving birth to 10 or more children and living in poverty. In the 1920s in the United States, over a million ordinary women wrote letters to their champion and supporter on birth control, Margaret Sanger (founder of the American Birth Control League). The following is part of a letter from a desperate woman quoted in Sanger's book *Woman and the New Race*:

> I have read in the paper about you and am very interested in Birth Control. I am a mother of four living children and one dead. . . . I would like you to advise me what to do to prevent from having any more as I would rather die than have another. . . . I've only got 2 rooms and kitchen and I do all my work and sewing which is very hard for me.

Finding these sources

The best way to see a diary extract or a letter is in its original form—for example, in an archive or a museum collection. However, you are more likely to be able to access them in a book or on the Internet. Because of this, it is important to find out who was involved in creating the version in front of you. Is the text you see in its original form? Did family members remove unflattering extracts before agreeing to its publication, or did editors take out parts that didn't suit the argument they wanted to present?

Examining letters and diaries

The other thing to consider when examining letters and diaries is to think about whom the writer was writing for. Letters are written to someone else, so it is easy to see how this might have influenced the writer. For example, a woman writing to a friend might be more open than she would be writing a letter to a stranger or an official. However, although diaries are written for oneself, many people wrote them knowing that they might be read in the future and tried to present themselves in a certain way.

Diary details

This is a section from a diary written by Mabel Lincoln, a housewife in Australia, in May 1930:

> Rise 7:30 Kornies [a kind of cereal] & toast, no eggs to be procured in the town, tidy up generally get to washing 11 o'clock, for dinner we have Puree made from Rice & beans I have in the meat safe & Mutton stock, boiled potatoes (in skins), tin kippered [canned salted] herrings, Tapioca warmed up (left from Yesterday) do three coppers [large boilers] full of white washing, finish at 5 PM cook scones & jam tarts for tea (pastry scraps left from yesterday makes 15 tarts) cook corn beef for tomorrow (Harold's favorite dish) . . .

When we first read this it sounds as if Lincoln only has two interests in life: housework and cooking! However, Australian history researcher Katie Holmes read this diary with a clear sense of its historical context. In the 1930s in Australia, there was a change in the amount of advice given to women from "experts" about "home economics" (cooking, housekeeping, and child-rearing). With this in mind, and knowing that Lincoln expected her diary might be read, we can see that she was eager to present herself as a good cook, housekeeper, wife, and mother. It tells us as much about the change in expectations of women in Australia at that time as it does about Lincoln herself.

Moving images

Here we look at how you can use moving images to research and answer questions about women in history, such as "Why did many women feel frustrated with their lives in the 1950s?" or "What can you say about the treatment of women workers after the end of World War II?" After World War II, there was a major shift in the way women were treated, and moving images—such as movies and TV advertisements—are one way of examining this change. You can watch old movies by borrowing DVDs or watching when they are shown on TV. To find out which might be the most interesting or relevant, read reviews of some of the era's movies in a movie guidebook or on the Internet. You can also search for ads and other film clips on websites such as YouTube.

Watch and learn

Many TV and movie advertisements in the early 1950s show women in the home being happy wives and mothers. The question a researcher needs to ask in this case is: What image of women were they trying to promote and why? Advertisers promoted the image of ideal women being housewives partly because governments wanted women to leave the world of work so men could have their jobs back. For advertisers this was also an opportunity to sell products, such as the latest electrical gadgets, to make the "happy home" complete.

We can also see the influence of the changing role of women in movies of the time. For example, the movie *Mildred Pierce* (1945) is about a woman who tries to succeed in business as a single parent, but ends up losing everything. What kind of message do you think this negative portrayal sent out to ambitious women in the United States and elsewhere?

Tips on evaluating moving images

When evaluating moving images, remember the 5 Ws: What, Who, When, Where, and Why.

- What kind of image is it? Is it an advertisement or propaganda designed to persuade us of an opinion?
- Who made the images? Is it a company selling a lifestyle in order to sell goods, or is the movie company reflecting a time or mood in its stories?
- When was it made? Was it made at the time of the events it portrays?
- Where was it made? What was going on in that place at the time?
- Why was it made? What were the filmmakers hoping to achieve?

*This is a **still** from "I Love Lucy," a hugely popular TV show in the 1950s and 1960s. Lucy's world is a cozy, domestic one, and images like this were thought to encourage women back into the home and away from the office. While not all women followed this role model, statistics show that there was a general shift. The average age at which women were married at this time was 20—the youngest it had been for 60 years.*

Newspapers and magazines

Newspaper reports are fairly easy primary sources to locate. Many articles are available online or on microfiche/film at libraries and archives. You can search the archives section of specific newspaper or magazine websites (such as that of *Time* magazine), or you can do a more general Internet search for articles on specific themes. Many newspapers and magazines claim to give facts, but is this always the case? You need to assess the texts you read to figure out whether, for example, they really are factual, or whether they are argument, persuasion, or even **propaganda**.

Always consider the following points:

- Different newspapers target people with particular backgrounds and views. Some newspapers are **right-wing**, or conservative, while others may be more **left-wing**, or liberal, in their views. This means that while most of the facts given in them may be correct, editors may have only selected certain facts or given the facts out of context to present a particular view.
- Some newspapers select stories because they are sensational and exciting, and therefore more likely to sell papers.
- Daily newspapers have to produce reports quickly. Reporters don't always have time to put their "facts" through a thorough checking procedure.

How to evaluate a newspaper report

The style of writing and choice of words (particularly of adjectives) in a report can help us understand its bias. Here are two newspaper reports printed in June 1913 after the death of Emily Davison. Davison was a militant British suffragette who died at a horse race after throwing herself in front of a horse owned by the king. These reports show the different reactions to the event in the right-wing press (*The Times*), whose readers were mainly against the suffragettes, and a left-wing newspaper (the *Manchester Guardian*), whose readers were likely to be more supportive. As you read, look at the underlined adjectives. Did the use of words like "reckless," "wanton," "wicked," and "unbalanced" in *The Times* article reflect or help shape public opinion at the time?

The Times

A deed of this kind, we need hardly say, is not likely to increase the popularity of any cause with the ordinary public. Reckless fanaticism is not regarded by them as a qualification for the franchise. . . . They say that the persons who wantonly destroy property and endanger innocent lives must be either desperately wicked or entirely unbalanced.

The Manchester Guardian

IMPRESSIVE LONDON PROCESSION

The procession, which was an impressive pageant, was watched by dense crowds. . . . Nearly five thousand members from all parts of the country marched in undisturbed quiet and orderliness behind the coffin. Perhaps what impressed the London mind in it all was the note of color. Among the women who walked there were hundreds dressed in black, but at the head was a young girl in yellow silk carrying a gilt cross.

Making myths

In the 1960s and 1970s, different groups of women were involved with the Women's Liberation Movement, campaigning on different issues, including equal pay, discrimination, and the overemphasis on women's appearance. To publicize their cause, one group of women demonstrated at the Miss America Pageant in 1968. They had planned to burn a selection of things, but city officials asked them not to, so instead they symbolically put some high-heeled shoes, bras, false eyelashes, and issues of women's beauty magazines in a trash can. One newspaper ran a headline about women burning bras, and the myth of bra-burning feminists was born. Why do you think the papers did this? Was it to make a more dramatic-sounding story, perhaps, or to trivialize the women's arguments?

In the late 1970s, these Canadian women celebrated International Women's Day by burning a bra. Were they responding to the media myth?

Back to books

Books—both fiction and nonfiction—often reflect what is going on in a society. The history researcher can therefore look at how the subject matter of books changes over a period of time for evidence of shifts in society. For example, the huge change in subject matter by some women writers in the 1970s is a marker of change in women's roles. Until the 1970s, many of the books aimed at women were about child-rearing or how to be a good housekeeper. In the 1970s, feminist and mainstream female writers flourished. Many of these books reflect the change away from the emphasis in the 1950s on women being good wives and mothers toward finding fulfillment in other ways, perhaps through careers. For example, in her book *The Feminine Mystique* (1963), Betty Friedan described her vision of the limited life of the suburban housewife as "a comfortable concentration camp," and in Germaine Greer's book *The Female Eunuch* (1970), the author likened marriage to a form of slavery.

The Feminine Mystique

Millions of women read *The Feminine Mystique* ("mystique" means a distinctive interest, mystery, or meaning surrounding a person or thing), and it is often credited with having started the second wave of feminism in the United States. Shown at right are the opening lines from *The Feminine Mystique*. The "problem," as Friedan sees it, is that many women are unfulfilled by their role as housewives. How do her words bring attention to the **stereotyping** of women and the difficulties she felt women faced in a changing world?

"The problem lay buried, unspoken for many years in the minds of American women. It was a strange stirring, a sense of dissatisfaction, a yearning that women suffered in the middle of the twentieth century in the United States. Each suburban housewife struggled with it alone. As she made the beds, shopped for groceries, matched slipcover material, ate peanut butter sandwiches with her children, chauffeured Cub Scouts and Brownies . . . she was afraid to ask even of herself the silent question: Is this all?"

Evaluation and variety

Remember, whatever form of resource you are using, to question it using the 5 Ws to evaluate usefulness and any bias. Research a variety of sources, from legal records to newspaper reports, and from letters to movies, to get a broad understanding of the period you are studying. Sources that may include more opinions than facts still contain useful information and can give you a real sense of people's feelings and motivations. Look at diaries, movies, and books within the context in which they were written to gain a deeper understanding of what they have to say.

Pseudonyms

Pseudonyms are "pen" or false names that authors sometimes use if they don't want to reveal their true identity. In the 19th century, many women writers wrote under male names in order to get published or for their words to be taken seriously, especially because women were expected to write only about romantic or domestic subjects. For example, the famous Victorian novelist George Eliot's real name was Mary Ann Evans. Some female authors still write under pseudonyms today. Joanne Rowling, author of the Harry Potter books, was asked by Bloomsbury, her publisher, to use two initials, J. K., instead of her first name because they feared that boys might be reluctant to read books written by a female author.

Betty Friedan's book, The Feminine Mystique, *made her an important figure in the U.S. women's movement of the 1960s and 1970s. Here Friedan takes part in a 1978 demonstration in support of the Equal Rights Amendment (ERA).*

Using Your Research

Research can be fascinating, and it is tempting to keep going as you discover more and more interesting facts, information, and opinions about a topic. At some point, however, you need to stop doing the research and start using it to answer your question or write your report. Now it is time to organize your research notes, sort out what you need and what you can use, and put it all together in a clear, meaningful way. Is that easier said than done?

Organizing the notes

First, clear some time and space to organize your notes. This stage is essential because it will help you to avoid repeating or missing bits of information. It will make life a lot easier for you when you start to plan and write your piece, so try to do it when there are no distractions around. You can organize your notes in a number of different ways. You can organize notes chronologically, for example. This is according to the date when things happened. Or you could organize the information within topics, such as "women in politics," "women at work," and "women's education."

Tips on sorting your notes

If you already have a rough idea of how your argument might progress in your essay or report, you could start to group your notes within sections that reflect those ideas. For example:

Ideas	*Notes*
1. Why the suffragettes fought for the right to vote.	
2. What tactics they used.	
3. Who opposed this change and why.	
4. When and why suffrage for women was won.	

Keeping balance

As you gather your research notes together, you may find you have some pieces of conflicting information. As long as you represent both sides of the argument, it is perfectly acceptable to quote different viewpoints in your report, because this gives balance to your writing and a richer view of the past. For example, when discussing the suffragette issue, be clear that you understand that some men supported the women's movement and some women were against the women's movement. Even female activists did not necessarily want to help *all* women—many early suffragists were fighting for the right to vote for middle- and upper-class women only, not working-class women. Keeping a balance like this avoids oversimplification of issues and proves that you have carried out wide-ranging research.

Organizing information in sections that are clearly headed and logically divided makes it easier to find things. It also saves you time when you need to pull the notes together into an essay. Having a large pile of notes can be daunting and confusing, while organizing them puts you in control of your work and helps you to be clear about how to progress.

Using graphic organizers

Graphic organizers help you to organize facts and information. This in turn will help you to express your ideas more successfully when you combine the notes in your final piece. Graphic organizers, as their name suggests, organize information in a graphic, or visual, way. There have been a variety of organizers throughout this book, such as the Venn diagram on page 9 and the timeline on page 27. They can be used in different ways. For example, Venn diagrams are useful for comparing and contrasting information, and timelines are useful for comparing and contrasting events in time and for putting events into their historical context.

Fishbone maps

Most graphic organizers use keywords or short sentences to fit information into a hierarchy of main or focus topic, subtopics, and details. A fishbone map is useful when a research topic has multiple strands, or elements. The idea of a fishbone map is that the central bone, or line, of the fish "skeleton" is your main idea or the point you wish to prove. This central bone has other bones coming off it that each contains a major argument about the main idea. These first ribs of the map can then have other lines coming off them to further expand a point or idea.

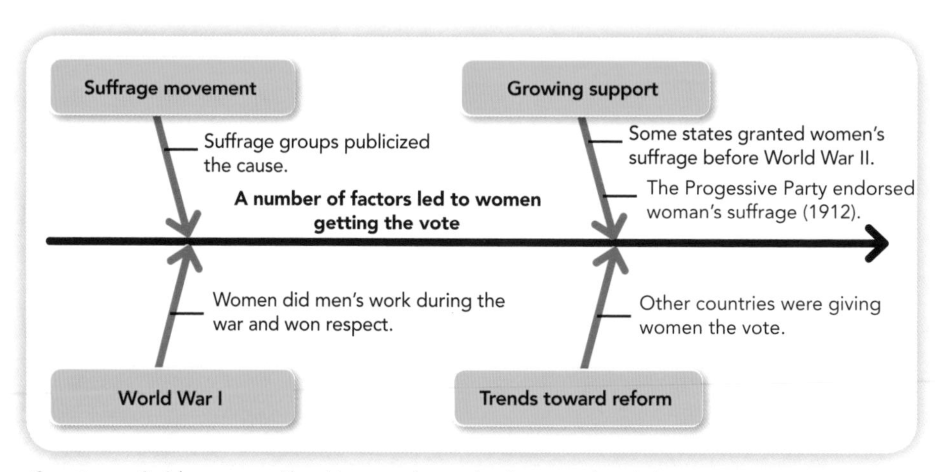

Creating a fishbone map, like this one about the factors that led to women getting the vote, helps you to organize information and be clear about the main issues.

Concept webs

A concept web or map is like a spider's web. There is one main heading or question in the middle. Leading out from this are various other strands, which contain the main ideas that are connected to the central theme or that answer the central question. From each of these subheadings come other bubbles or boxes that contain supporting facts and details. Organizing facts in a web like this prepares you for writing. In this case, the facts will help prepare an answer to the question: Why was the women's movement so active in the late 1960s and the 1970s?

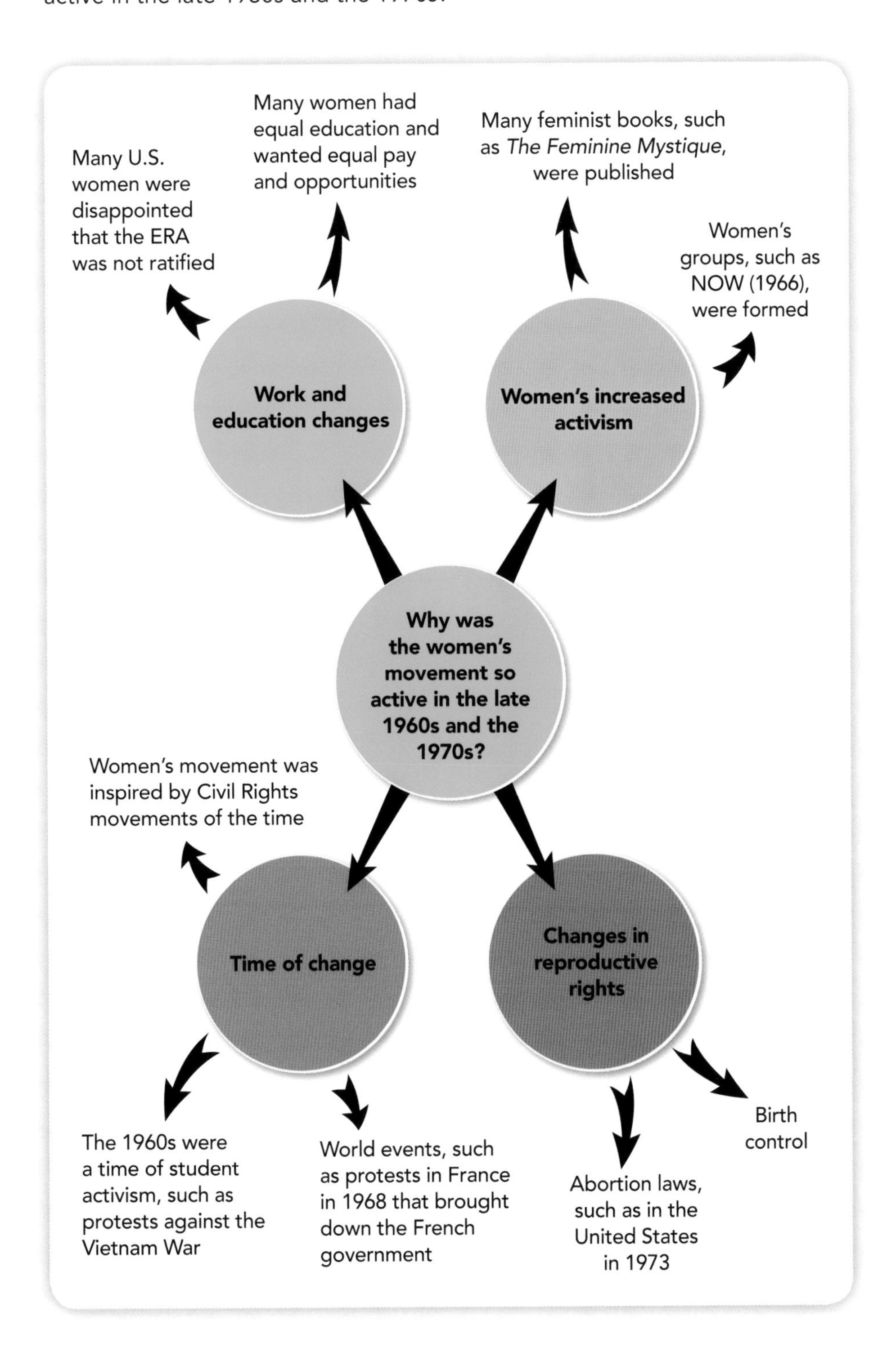

Planning your written work or presentation

Once you have sorted out your notes and made a graphic organizer to organize your thoughts, the next step is planning how to formulate your presentation or write your report or essay answer. For most written projects, you should include at least four clear sections: an introduction, the main text containing your evidence and information, a conclusion, and endmatter, such as a list of sources.

Introduction

The introduction can take various forms. Many students use it to outline what their argument will be and how they will explain it. Just because this is first in your plan doesn't mean you have to write it first. Some people prefer to write the introduction after they have completed the rest.

Main section

The main section of the essay usually consists of a number of paragraphs, or subheadings, within which you will develop your argument. Ideally you will plan what will go in each section before you begin writing. That way, you can check that you have sufficient evidence and examples to demonstrate your points. At this point you can also decide where you need to present alternative points of view.

Conclusion

In the conclusion, you should recap the key points of your argument and sum up your final thoughts. The endmatter is more straightforward, but there are conventions you usually have to follow when presenting book lists or giving references for quotes (see page 50).

Tips for biographies

Your work may take a different form for different kinds of reports and presentations. For example, if you are working on a biography, you need to address the following questions:

- Who is the person you are writing about (age, background, and so on)?
- What events changed this person?
- What made this person famous or important?
- Why did this person in particular achieve what he or she did?
- How was this person important to other people?

What are the key differences between women's role in 1900 and today?

I. Women's role in the home has changed since 1900.

A. The size of families has changed.
   1. In 1900 women had large families.
   2. Today, most families in the West have no more than two children due to birth control (laws and dates).

B. Women's position at home has changed.
   1. In 1900 most middle-class women lived at home until they were married.
   2. Many women today live independently.

C. Women's housework
   1. In 1900 women ran the household.
   2. Today, working men and women share more of the household duties, but in reality women still do the major share.

II. Women's options for occupations have changed.

A. In 1900 women had a limited choice of jobs.
   1. Most women in 1900 who worked did so as servants or in manual labor for low pay.
   2. Women mostly did not do the same jobs as men because the general belief was they were less capable and less intelligent.

B. In theory women can enter any occupation today.
   1. There are few women in the top jobs in their chosen profession.
   2. There is still resistance to females working in some traditionally male jobs.
   3. Although women have the right to equal pay, their pay is still often lower than men's.

III. Women's rights have changed.

A. Women's rights to education have changed.
   1. In 1900 few women had the right to further education.
   2. Women in the West have equal right to further education.

B. Women's rights in law have changed.
   1. In 1900 few women had the right to vote and had few legal rights.
   2. Today, women have the right to vote, and there are laws giving them equality.

One way to plan the paragraphs you wish to include in the main body of your text, or in your oral report or presentation, is to use an outline like this. This breaks a topic down into main ideas with subheadings that contain sentences about supporting facts or details. The sections are prompts for the organization of your work. Don't forget to back up the statements with facts, examples, and quotations.

Write it!

When you are finally ready to write your written project or essay, you should be able to follow your plan, and your work will automatically have a sensible structure. That leaves you free to make it fluent and interesting, with a lot of examples from your research. Try to make your text factual and explanatory. Back up clear statements and arguments with evidence and examples.

You can and should use examples of other people's persuasive texts, such as opinions in letters or quotes from advertisements, but you need to try to give a balanced argument. To communicate your ideas successfully, try to write clearly. Divide the work into paragraphs and try not to make your sentences too long or too complex.

How to use quotes

You can use quotations to illustrate a point, to add credibility or support to your argument, and to show that your ideas are based on careful research. You can integrate short quotes into your main text in quotation marks. For example: "Women in World War II learned to do men's work, as Annice Gibbs, who worked for the British WLA Timber Corps, remarked: 'After our training, we soon got used to heavy work, such as lifting pit-props and cutting them into various lengths for the coal mines.'"

Start longer quotes on a new line and include the author's last name, the year when the book or article was published, and the page on which you found it in the text, as a footnote, or in an endnote list.

The perils of plagiarism

Any report, exam, or essay with your name on it is yours, and you should write it in your own words, using your own research and understanding. **Plagiarism** is when someone copies another person's material and passes it off as his or her own and does not credit the original author. Copying from someone else's assignment or handing in an essay you downloaded from the Internet is plagiarism.

Some schools and colleges expel students for plagiarism. This is another reason to keep a record of your research sources and quote them properly.

Using illustrations

Another way to add interest and variety to your work is to include illustrations. However, any pictures you use should add something to your argument and should not be purely decorative!

Carefully chosen pictures extend the information in the text. Include new information in picture captions, rather than just repeating ideas you have already covered in the main text. (See copyright issues involved with using pictures on page 32.)

Here is an example of how a picture can be used to reinforce and extend information in a text. This picture and the caption with it are intended to accompany text in a written report about the way that women increased their share of the workforce in most countries of the world during the 1970s and 1980s.

This is a sample caption: "In history, women's clothes often mirrored their function in the world. For example, in 1900 women still wore long, confining dresses that echoed the fact that their lives were often confined to their homes. In the 1980s, many women were increasing their power in the workplace, and feminized versions of male business suits with wide shoulder pads became very popular."

Always check and edit!

Leaving work until the last minute is not only stressful, it may also mean you don't get a chance to check and edit it. This would be a mistake, because checking and editing is a very important stage in the process. Before handing in any major piece of work, try to give yourself a day or two to re-read and correct it. It might also help to ask a friend or family member to go over it, too, to see if there are any places where it doesn't make sense or where a point isn't fully explained. This is also your chance to reduce the text if it is too long, or to add a paragraph if it is coming in below the expected word count. As you read through your work, make sure that it is organized into clear paragraphs or sections that are clearly related to each other.

Endmatter

The "endmatter" in a written piece of work should consist of a list of references cited and a bibliography. The bibliography is a list of the books, magazines, websites, and other resources you used in your research, while the list of endnotes cites the specifics of the sources you have used—for example, where you found a quotation. In both cases you need to give information on the title, the author, the publisher, and the date of publication. In endnotes or footnotes you should also give the page number where the material you used occurs. When quoting sources from the Internet, give the reader enough information to locate the site easily. For example, give the author's name and the full website address. Ask your teacher for the exact format required for bibliography and endnote citations.

Presentation matters

The way you present your work matters. A well-presented work is clearer and easier to read and understand and therefore more likely to be understood and given a good grade. Here are tips for a good presentation. If you feel you need further help, don't hesitate to ask your teacher.

Written presentation tips

- Take time to sort and organize your notes using graphic organizers.
- Plan your assignment carefully, perhaps using a graphic outline.
- Use clear, descriptive headings.
- Structure the main part of your assignment using paragraphs and developing an argument thoughtfully.
- Write in your own words and use your own balanced arguments.
- Choose quotes that support your argument.
- Include a bibliography of your research sources.
- Check, edit, and refine your work before handing it in.

- Check for spelling errors.
- Read it out loud to check that the sentences are clear and that there aren't any missing words.
- Check your punctuation. Errors in punctuation can change the sense and meaning of a phrase or sentence.
- Make sure your references (footnotes or endnotes) and bibliography are consistent and complete.

The last word

After you turn in your assignment and are thinking about the great grade you are likely to get after all your hard work, there is no need to stop doing research. People research to write a particular essay or report, but they also research out of personal interest and a desire to be better informed. If the topic you have been working on really has gripped your imagination, you may find that you want to continue reading and learning about it for a long time afterward.

While some people in the West think of Muslim women as oppressed, women under the laws of the Qur'an have long had some rights that were only granted to western women in the 19th and 20th centuries, such as the right to education and to own property. Researching information like this can help create balance in reports and presentations.

Glossary

abortion termination of a pregnancy

artifact human-made object that gives us clues about how people lived in the past

biased influenced or prejudiced against someone or something

bibliography list of books or other texts usually giving the title, the author's name, the details of the publisher, and the date of publication

birth control method used to prevent pregnancy, such as taking a contraceptive pill

chronological arrangement of events in time order, from earliest to most recent

cite give credit to a work or author

contraception measures taken to prevent pregnancy

copyright legal right granted to an author or other person, for the exclusive publication or reproduction of his or her work

database online tool a researcher can use, containing information from a range of sources and links that are selected and developed for a specific audience. Most are subscription services that require membership or payment.

graphic organizer visual representation of knowledge, concepts, or ideas

illiterate unable to read or write

index alphabetical listing of names and topics that appear inside a book, along with page numbers where they appear

left-wing in politics, usually associated with people or policies that place the needs of the community above the short-term wants of the individual

maternity leave mother's paid or unpaid time off work to care for a new baby

oppressed when a person or group of people are governed or treated cruelly or unjustly

paraphrase your own version of information that you have read, rewritten in your own words

plagiarism when someone copies and presents someone else's writing as his or her own work

primary source manuscript, record, or document that provides original or "firsthand" research or documentation

propaganda promotion of ideas, often using a selective version of the truth

quote/quotation copy of words of text originally published elsewhere. Direct quotations usually appear in quotation marks.

ratify give official approval to something. An amendment to the U.S. Constitution needs to be ratified by three-quarters of the 50 states.

right legal or moral entitlement

right-wing in politics, usually associated with people or policies that favor individual interests over the community, and tradition over change

scanning reading technique used to find specific information quickly. You glance across a page looking for specific words, subheads, and images.

secondary source research material or source that contains information that has been quoted, translated, or based upon another primary or original source

skimming reading technique to find out what a source contains. You read titles, introductions or first paragraphs, first sentences of every other paragraph, picture captions, and summaries or last paragraphs.

SQ3R stands for Survey, Question, Read, Recite, Review. This technique guides you through finding the relevance of evidence and also remembering it through reading and reciting.

stereotype oversimplified image or representation

still single film frame from a movie or TV show used like a photograph

suffrage right to vote

suffragette woman who campaigned for the right of women to vote. Suffragettes were more militant (hands-on and forceful) than suffragists and were willing to break the law to make their views heard.

suffragist person who campaigned for the right of women to vote

summary sentence or paragraph that sums up a selection of information

UN short for United Nations, an international organization of independent states formed in 1945 to promote peace and security

western world political name for rich, industrialized, mainly democratically governed countries, such as those of Europe and North America

Find Out More

Books

Adams, Colleen. *Women's Suffrage: A Primary Source History of the Women's Rights Movement in America.* New York: Rosen, 2003.

Bausum, Ann. *With Courage and Cloth: Winning the Fight for a Woman's Right to Vote.* Washington, D.C.: National Geographic, 2004.

Donlan, Leni. *American History Through Primary Sources: The Struggle for Women's Right to Vote.* Chicago: Raintree, 2008.

Gorman, Jacqueline Laks. *Trailblazers of the Modern World: Gloria Steinem.* Milwaukee: World Almanac Education, 2004.

Price, Sean. *Front-Page Lives: Benazir Bhutto.* Chicago: Heinemann Library, 2010.

Ross, Mandy. *20th Century Perspectives: The Changing Role of Women.* Chicago: Heinemann Library, 2002.

Websites

At www.pbs.org/stantonanthony, there is an interesting website about the movie *Not for Ourselves Alone*, which tells the stories of early U.S. feminists Elizabeth Cady Stanton and Susan B. Anthony and tracks key events in the suffrage movement, shows historic documents and essays, and takes a look at where women are today.

The U.S. National Organization of Women has its own website, www.now.org, on which you can read pages about its history.

The National Women's History Museum website has information and primary sources about the history of the U.S. suffrage movement, as well as a lot of images from the period, at www.nwhm.org/exhibits/intro.html.

The Library of Congress has photos and videos linked to women and war and the effects of war on women's lives, at www.loc.gov/vets/stories/ex-war-womenatwar.html.

The UN website "WomenWatch," at www.un.org/womenwatch, has information and resources on gender equality and female empowerment.

Places to visit

The International Museum of Women in San Francisco, California, combines exhibits that celebrate and chronicle the history of women's roles in society and history; see www.imow.org.

The Library of Congress houses a vast collection related to U.S. women's history. Access is free and open to everyone. For details of the collection, see http://memory.loc.gov/ammem/awhhtml/index.html.

Artifacts

At www.nwhm.org/exhibits/gallery_1.html (National Women's History Museum), there is an image gallery in which you can view items such as suffrage ribbons and medals and other artifacts relating to women's changing role. There are also pages of text, pictures, and posters about the struggle for women's suffrage.

Ideas for topics to research

Here are some ideas for topics to research on the theme of the changing role of women:

- One interesting line of research would be the links between the civil rights movements and the women's rights movement, and the women involved.
- Find out more about individuals who played a major part in women's changing role in the 20th century, such as Alice Paul, Germaine Greer, Gloria Steinem, Betty Friedan, and others.
- Explore women's suffrage around the world, in India, China, and Japan, for example, or in Egypt, researching the Egyptian Feminist Union, founded in 1923.
- Look at women in politics, such as Eleanor Roosevelt, Indira Gandhi, Benazir Bhutto, Aung San Suu Kyi (elected leader of Burma in 1990, but not allowed to govern), and Hillary Clinton.
- Research the state of women's education throughout the 20th century, including the times when girls in different countries were granted the same education rights as boys.
- Research the rights and status of women in terms of marriage and divorce in different countries throughout the 20th century.
- Explore what roles women have played in the world of the media and the arts, and how this role has changed throughout the 20th century.

Index